Seashores

To the One who created seashores.

—*Genesis* 1:9

Ω

Published by
PEACHTREE PUBLISHERS
1700 Chattahoochee Avenue
Atlanta, Georgia 30318-2112
www.peachtree-online.com

Text © 2017 by Cathryn P. Sill
Illustrations © 2017 by John Sill

Illustrations created in watercolor on archival quality 100% rag paper
Text and titles set in Novarese from Adobe

Edited by Vicky Holifield

Printed in April 2017 by Imago in China
10 9 8 7 6 5 4 3 2 1
First Edition

Library of Congress Cataloging-in-Publication Data

Names: Sill, Cathryn P., 1953- author. | Sill, John, illustrator. | Sill,
  Cathryn P., 1953- About habitats.
Title: About habitats : seashores / written by Cathryn Sill ; illustrated by
  John Sill.
Description: First edition. | Atlanta, Georgia : Peachtree Publishers,
  [2016]. | Series: About habitats | Audience: Ages 3-7. | Audience: K to
  grade 3.
Identifiers: LCCN 2016030701 | ISBN 9781561459681
Subjects: LCSH: Seashore ecology—Juvenile literature. | Seashore
  Animals—Juvenile literature.
Classification: LCC QH541.5.S35 S528 2016 | DDC 577.69/9—dc23 LC record
available at *https://lccn.loc.gov*
2016030701

ABOUT HABITATS

Seashores

Written by **Cathryn Sill**   Illustrated by **John Sill**

Ω

PEACHTREE
ATLANTA

Seashores are the narrow strips of land that border the seas.

Seashores are found worldwide, where oceans meet the land.

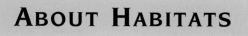

ABOUT HABITATS

Seashores

Seashores are the places where land and oceans meet.

There are different kinds of seashores all
around the world.

A.

B.

Many seashores have sandy beaches.

Sometimes huge piles of sand called "dunes" form on sandy beaches.

Some rocky shores have huge rocks at the edge of the water.

Other rocky shores have tall, steep cliffs.

Pebble beaches are covered with small, rounded rocks.

Mud covers some seashores.

Ocean tides cause the water on seashores to rise and fall.

a.

b.

Seashores are covered with water when the tide is high. Most of the shore is dry during low tide.

Strong waves and wind often pound seashores.

Plants have to be tough to live in the salty spray, strong winds, and hot sunshine at seashores.

Many kinds of animals find food and raise their babies on seashores.

a.

b.

d.

Some seashore animals stay in one place all their lives.

Some live in the sand.

PLATE 15
ATLANTIC OCEAN
SEASHORE

Coquina Clam
Lugworm
Mole Crab
Whimbrel

Others travel about looking for food and places to rest.

Seashores are important places that need
to be protected.

SEASHORES

Afterword

PLATE 1

All of the land on Earth is surrounded by ocean. Seashores, also called coastlines, are the narrow strips of land that border the sea. Earth's seashores are thousands of miles (kilometers) long but in many places are only a few yards (meters) wide. Seashores provide a habitat for many animals and plants. Silver Gulls are found near seashores in most of Australia and parts of New Zealand.

PLATE 2

Some seashores are located in areas where the weather is either hot or cold all year. Others are in places where summers are warm and winters are cold. No two seashores are exactly the same, and they are constantly changing. Many things—including waves, wind, tides, climate, and the type of rock on the shore—cause differences in seashores.

PLATE 3

Sand is formed when chunks of rock, shells, and coral are broken into smaller pieces by waves and weather. The pieces continue to break and wear down until they are tiny grains. Sandy beaches are always changing because the waves and winds constantly move the sand around. Sea turtles dig holes for nests on sandy beaches. Hawksbill Turtles are critically endangered because of overhunting for their meat, eggs, and beautiful shells. They live in the tropical waters of the Pacific, Atlantic, and Indian Oceans.

PLATE 4

Sand dunes are important parts of many beaches. They protect the land from high waves caused by storms. Grasses that grow on dunes have strong roots that help keep the sand in place. Some seashore animals find shelter and food in the dunes. Animals like Beach Mice and Gopher Tortoises live in the dunes along the Atlantic seashore in Florida. Development along the coast has caused a loss of habitat for both animals.

PLATE 5

Rocky shores are made of solid rock. They may be covered with large, flat ledges of rock or huge boulders. Some plants and animals live all their lives on rocky shores. Others, like Stellar Sea Lions, visit the shores to rest and raise their young. Stellar Sea Lions live in the northern Pacific Ocean from California to Japan. They are the largest type of sea lion.

PLATE 6

Steep cliffs along coastlines are made of hard rock that can stand against the pounding of the waves and wind. Sea cliffs provide safe nesting places for many seabirds. Predators have a hard time reaching nests built high on the cliffs. Northern Gannets spend most of their lives at sea in the Atlantic Ocean. They come to shore by the thousands to nest on cliffs in North America and Europe.

PLATE 7

Beaches covered with small to medium-sized pebbles are called "shingle beaches." Waves toss the stones around, making them smooth and rounded. The moving stones make it hard for plants to take root and survive on shingle beaches. Some birds, such as Common Ringed Plovers, nest on the pebbles above the wave action. Their eggs and babies are camouflaged to blend into the surrounding rocks. Common Ringed Plovers live in Europe, Asia, and parts of North America.

PLATE 8

Muddy seashores are usually located in sheltered places where waves are gentle. The mud is soft and provides a good habitat for many animals like worms, sea snails, and other mollusks. The animals buried in the mudflats provide food for shorebirds. Eurasian Oystercatchers live along seashores in Europe and Asia.

PLATE 9

The seashore has different zones between high and low tides. The splash zone is the area where waves splash on shore. The high tide zone is flooded only during high tides. The middle tide zone is wet when the tide rises and dry when it falls. The low tide zone is covered with water most of the time. Different species of animals are able to live in each zone.

PLATE 10

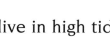

Animals that live in high tide zones are pounded by strong waves. Most of those that live on sandy beaches burrow down in the sand for protection as the water crashes above them. Animals in the middle tide zone are able to live both in and out of water. Rocky shores along the Pacific Coast of North America often have tide pools where animals such as sea anemones, sea stars, and mussels cling to the rocks. They search for tiny pieces of floating food while they are covered with water. Shellfish close their shells tightly for protection when the tide is low. Sea anemones pull their tentacles in and wait for the water to return. Some animals stay safe in the water that is trapped in tide pools.

PLATE 11

Waves are caused by wind blowing across the surface of the ocean. The powerful force of the wind and waves constantly wears away the rocks or moves the sand located along seashores. Red-billed Tropicbirds are ocean birds that come to rocky shores to raise their young. They nest above the crashing waves in cracks and holes in the cliffs. Red-billed Tropicbirds live in tropical areas in the Atlantic, Pacific, and Indian Oceans.

PLATE 12

Many seashore plants grow close to the ground for protection from the wind. Others have thick and waxy leaves that make it easier to store water. Some have leaves covered with tiny hairs that protect the plant from the heat. Pink Sand Verbenas have thick, water-storing leaves. They live in sandy soil along the western coast of North America.

PLATE 13

Some animals live on seashores all the time. Others just visit the shore. Marine Iguanas eat the algae that grow on the rocky shores of the Galapagos Islands. Sally Lightfoot Crabs live on rocky shores in the tropics and subtropics of North and South America. Gentoo Penguins nest on shores of the Southern Ocean. South African Fur Seals come to shores in South Africa to raise their babies. Northern Raccoons live inland in North America but sometimes come to the shores along the Atlantic and Pacific Oceans to hunt for food.

PLATE 14

Animals that always stay in one place are called "sessile." Adult acorn barnacles attach themselves to something hard like a rock and never change locations. They wave their feathery "legs" in the water to catch food as it floats by. When the tide is low, they close their shells tightly to keep from drying out. Titan Acorn Barnacles are native to the Pacific Coasts of North and South America. Their range has spread to parts of the Atlantic Ocean and to the Gulf of Mexico.

PLATE 15

Many seashore animals burrow into the cool, damp sand when the tide is out. This keeps them from drying out. Burrowing also helps some of them hide from shorebirds and other predators. Whimbrels hunt for buried animals by probing into the sand with their long bills. Coquina Clams, Mole Crabs, and Lugworms live on seashores along the eastern coast of the United States.

PLATE 16

Many shorebirds migrate hundreds or even thousands of miles (kilometers) each year. When they become tired and hungry during their long trip, they depend on seashores as stopping places along the way. Each spring, large flocks of Red Knots stop on the shores of Delaware Bay in the United States to feed on Horseshoe Crab eggs. They feast on the eggs for energy to complete their journey to their nesting grounds in the Arctic tundra. Red Knots live along shorelines around the world.

PLATE 17

Oil spills, garbage dumping, and other types of pollution harm seashores all over the world. Toxic chemicals from factories and farms are carried to seashores by rivers. Overdevelopment destroys the habitats of many animals and plants. Piping Plovers are listed as endangered because many of their nesting sites have been ruined by development and recreation. They nest on sandy beaches and sandflats along the Atlantic Coast, in the Great Plains, and around the Great Lakes of North America.

GLOSSARY

BIOME—an area such as a forest or wetland that shares the same types of plants and animals
ECOSYSTEM—a community of living things and their environment
HABITAT—the place where animals and plants live

camouflage—colors or patterns on an animal that help it hide
climate—the weather conditions of a place over a long period of time
development—the building of structures such as homes or businesses
endangered—threatened with becoming extinct (no longer existing)
mudflat—an area of muddy land covered by water at high tide
predator—an animal that lives by hunting and eating other animals
tropical—the area near the equator that is hot year-round

BIBLIOGRAPHY

BOOKS

EXPLORE AND DISCOVER: THE SEASHORE by Angela Wilkes (Kingfisher)
EYEWITNESS: SEASHORE by Steve Parker (DK Publishing)
PETERSON FIRST GUIDE TO SEASHORES by John C Kricher (Houghton Mifflin Company)
WORLD ABOUT US: SEASHORE by Kate Bedford (Stargazer Books)

WEBSITES

Missouri Botanical Garden
www.mbgnet.net

Biomes of the World
www.thewildclassroom.com/biomes/index.html